Oct

The Living Daylights

OXFORD
UNIVERSITY PRESS

Great Clarendon Street, Oxford, OX2 6DP, United Kingdom

Oxford University Press is a department of the University of Oxford.
It furthers the University's objective of excellence in research, scholarship,
and education by publishing worldwide. Oxford is a registered trade
mark of Oxford University Press in the UK and in certain other countries

First published in Dominoes 2016

2018 2017 2016

10 9 8 7 6 5 4 3 2 1

ISBN: 978 0 19 424895 2   Book
ISBN: 978 0 19 462843 3   Book and Audio Pack

Printed in China

This book is printed on paper from certified and well-managed sources

ACKNOWLEDGEMENTS

Cover reproduced with permission from: Getty Images (Gun Illustration EPS 10/
popay/Digitalvision Vectors); Shutterstock (Gold Bars 1000 grams/ktsdesign).

Illustrations by: Gavin Reece

The publisher would like to thank the following for permission to reproduce photographs:
Alamy Images p58 (Helen Shapiro, 1966/Pictorial Press Ltd); Corbis pp12
(Austrian Alps/Peter Barritt/Robert Harding World Imagery), 46 (Police
officers at West German border/dpa), 58 (Woman wearing mini dress, 1966/
Bettmann), 58 (The Beatles, 1964/Hulton-Deutsch Collection), 60 (1948 Land
Rover/Car Culture), 60 (Couples dancing, 1941/Bettmann); Getty Images
pp60 (De Havilland Comet/Fox Photos), 60 (Vera Lynn, 1945/Kurt Hutton),
60 (George Formby, 1940/Redferns); Kobal Collection pp58 (The Sound of
Music/20th Century Fox), 60 (Henry V (1944)/ITV Global); Shutterstock pp13
(Gold bullion/James Steidl), 58 (Mini vintage car/f9photos).

DOMINOES

Series Editors: Bill Bowler and Sue Parminter

Octopussy
&
The Living Daylights

Ian Fleming

Text adaptation by Nick Bullard

Illustrated by Gavin Reece

Ian Fleming was born in London in 1908. He studied at Eton, and in Austria and Germany. He worked first as a journalist, and then at a London financial company. During World War Two, he went to work for British Naval Intelligence. This experience inspired his later James Bond stories. Fleming married in 1952. In the same year, at home in Jamaica, he wrote his first Bond adventure, *Casino Royale*. It was published in 1953, and was very successful. Thirteen more Bond books followed, and there have been many Bond films since then. Fleming died in 1964. The short stories *Octopussy* and *The Living Daylights* were first published together in 1966. Learn more about Ian Fleming at www.ianfleming.com

IAN FLEMING PUBLICATIONS LIMITED

OXFORD
UNIVERSITY PRESS

BEFORE READING

1 **These people and animals are in the story *Octopussy*. Match each sentence with a picture. Use a dictionary to help you.**

1 Major Dexter Smythe

2 Octopussy

3 James Bond

4 The Foo brothers

5 a scorpion fish

6 Hannes Oberhauser

a ☐ This Austrian mountain guide is good at climbing.

b ☐ This animal has dangerous spines. It can kill a man in minutes.

c ☐ These businesspeople buy and sell gold.

d ☐ This soldier killed a man and stole some gold just after World War 2 (1939-45).

e ☐ This person works for the British Secret Service.

f ☐ This animal lives in a coral reef, and eats fish.

2 **Four of these people or animals die in the story. Which four, do you think? Write their names here.**

....

OCTOPUSSY

CHAPTER I

IN THE WATERS OFF JAMAICA

12TH AUGUST 1965, EARLY AFTERNOON

'Good afternoon, Octopussy,' said **Major** Dexter **Smythe** to the **octopus**. 'I'm going to bring you something special today.'

He stood up in the water. It came to the top of his arms. He took off his **mask**, washed it in the sea, and put it back on. Then he put his head down under the water again.

The octopus was like an old brown bag with an eye. The eye was watching Major Smythe carefully from a hole in the **coral**. He saw the end of a small **tentacle** come out of the hole. It moved around in the water. The major smiled. Perhaps in a month or two they could be friends. But he didn't have a month. He could put his hand down now – to the tentacle. To shake hands.

Major an important officer in the army

Smythe /smaɪð/

octopus an animal that lives in the sea and has eight arms

mask something that you wear over your face when you swim under the water

coral a hard thing in the sea; it is made of the bodies of little sea animals

tentacle the soft arm of an octopus

'No, Octopussy,' thought Major Smythe. 'No hand yet. You have seven more tentacles. You can pull me down into the water too easily. Not now. Perhaps later.' Major Smythe swam off, through the coral. He was looking for a **scorpion fish**.

Major Dexter Smythe was once in the British army. Now he was fifty-four years old, fat, and he had a very bad **heart**. With his heart, he knew that he would die soon, and he didn't worry about it much. After the death of his wife, Mary, two years earlier, he had nobody to love, nothing to live for. He had no real friends, and he didn't want any now. He was bored with life. His only interests were the sea beside his house in Jamaica, the coral **reef**, and the fish. He really loved the fish with their beautiful colours. He talked to them while he swam.

'Good afternoon, Gregory, and how are you today? Hello, Blue Boy, you're too fat these days.'

He loved all the fish, and perhaps they loved him. He had only one enemy on the reef – the scorpion fish.

Scorpion fish live in most of the warm waters of the world. The West Indian scorpion fish is usually about thirty centimetres long, and up to 500 grams. It is one of the worst-looking fish in the sea, with its brown-grey body, heavy head, and angry red eyes. It has a big mouth, strong teeth, and dangerous **spines** on its back. The spines have a strong **poison**, tetrodotoxin, in them. This can kill a person in a few minutes. The scorpion fish is the most dangerous thing for any swimmer in the waters off Jamaica. Its brown-grey colour means that it is often hard to see next to the **rocks**. Major Smythe wanted to catch one with his **spear** and give it to Octopussy.

'Will Octopussy eat the scorpion fish,' he thought, 'or will the poison kill the octopus? Will Octopussy eat the body but not the spines? I don't want Octopussy to die, but I must know the answer. And I must know it today, before they take me back to London!'

Then Major Smythe thought unhappily about that conversation earlier in the day. A conversation which meant **arrest**, and prison in England for life.

scorpion fish a very dangerous kind of fish that can kill you

heart this is in your chest; it sends the blood round your body

reef a large wall of coral under the water

spine a long, hard part of an animal's body that can hurt you

poison something that can kill you when it gets into your body

rock a very big stone

spear a long, thin stick with a sharp knife at one end that you use for killing fish under the water

arrest when the police catch a person after they do something wrong; to catch a person after they do something wrong

The day started as usual. Major Smythe woke up late, took his heart **pills**, had a **shower**, and a little breakfast. He never ate much in the morning, and he spent an hour giving the rest of his breakfast to the birds in his garden. Then he took more of his heart pills, and sat down to read the newspaper. At 10.30, he heard a car drive up to the front of the house. Major Smythe hurried into the bedroom and put on a white shirt. Then he went to meet his visitor.

When he saw the tall man at the door – with his dark hair, and his cold, blue-grey eyes – Major Smythe knew that there was a **problem**. This man was from the police, or the army, he could see. Twenty years before, the major **smuggled** something into England. Perhaps they knew about this now. But how?

pill a small, round thing that a doctor gives you to eat when you are ill

shower water comes out of this; you stand under it to clean your body

problem something that happens which makes things difficult for you

smuggle to take things out of a country secretly

3

'Good morning, Major Smythe. My name's Bond, James Bond. I'm from the **Ministry of Defence**.' Bond did not shake hands.

'Ah, the **Secret Service**?' said Major Smythe, smiling. He knew that the answer was yes.

Bond didn't reply to the question. 'Can we talk?' he said.

'Of course. In the garden, or the house – which do you prefer?' answered the major.

'The house is fine,' said Bond.

They went into the living room, and Major Smythe sat down. Bond stood by the window.

'So,' said Major Smythe, 'what can I do for you? I haven't worked for a long time, but I'm always happy to help. Are there problems here on Jamaica?'

'No,' said Bond. 'I'm here to ask you about your time with the Secret Service in 1945. I'm very interested in your work in Austria after the end of the Second World War.'

'Ah yes, I remember. Are you writing a book about those days?'

'No,' said Bond. 'I'm only interested in one thing. Do you remember a village called Ober Aurach, near **Kitzbühel** in Austria?'

'Oh yes, that was an interesting job,' said the major. 'We caught a group of German secret policemen there. They were hiding in the village. We sent them all to a prison in Munich. They left a big box of **documents** behind, and we looked through them, and then sent them to our office in Salzburg. After that, we went on to the next village.'

'You were the only British soldier there who spoke German. So you read the documents. Did you send them all to Salzburg?' Bond asked him.

'Of course,' replied Major Smythe. 'There was nothing very exciting – papers with names and addresses on them, and other things like that.'

Bond thought for a minute. 'Do you remember Hannes Oberhauser?' he asked.

It was a really hot morning, but Major Smythe suddenly felt very cold. 'Sorry. I don't think so,' he answered.

'Strange,' said Bond. 'On the day that you found the documents, you asked the people at your hotel for the name of the best mountain **guide** in Kitzbühel. They told you about Oberhauser. The next day, you asked for a day's holiday. You went to Oberhauser's house, arrested him, and drove him away in a car. Do you remember him now?'

'I'm sorry. I don't remember the name. It was a long time ago,' the major said.

'Oberhauser had grey hair, and a bad leg. He spoke some English because he taught people to **ski** before the war,' Bond went on.

'No, I don't remember a skiing teacher,' said Major Smythe.

'Your gun at that time was a Webley & Scott .45. Number 8967/362,' Bond said.

'Well, I had a Webley,' said Major Smythe. 'Not a very good gun. But I don't remember the number.'

'The number's right,' Bond told him.

'I'm sorry,' said Major Smythe. 'But why are you here?'

'You know why,' said Bond. 'Now, Major, I'm going out into the garden for ten minutes. You think about things. I know what happened, but I want to hear your side of it. You see, I visited the Foo brothers in Kingston yesterday.'

Bond walked into the garden. Major Smythe was thinking hard. So Bond knew about the Foo brothers. Then there was no hope for him!

guide someone who shows other people where to go

ski to go over snow fast on long, flat pieces of wood

READING CHECK

Are these sentences true or false? Tick the boxes.

		True	False
a	Major Smythe loves swimming in the sea.	☑	☐
b	Octopussy has poison in its body.	☐	☐
c	Smythe wants to give a scorpion fish to Octopussy.	☐	☐
d	Smythe has a problem with his back.	☐	☐
e	James Bond wants to talk to Smythe about Octopussy.	☐	☐
f	Smythe was in Austria in 1945.	☐	☐
g	Smythe speaks German.	☐	☐
h	Hannes Oberhauser was a secret policeman.	☐	☐

WORD WORK

1 These words don't match the pictures. Correct them.

a ~~spear~~ ...*octopus*...

b heart...................

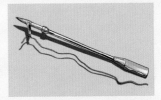

c rock...................

d octopus...................

e reef...................

f tentacle...................

g pills...................

h mask...................

2 Complete the puzzle with other new words from Chapter 1. What is the word in the blue squares?

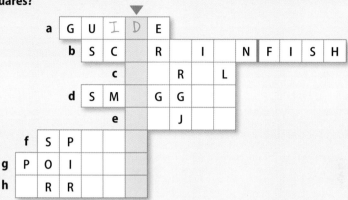

The word in the blue squares is: . . . .

GUESS WHAT

What happens in the next chapter? Tick two boxes.

a ☐ James Bond shows Major Smythe his old gun.

b ☐ Hannes Oberhauser comes to Smythe's house.

c ☐ Smythe tells Bond about some gold.

d ☐ The Foo brothers come to Smythe's house.

e ☐ Smythe tells Bond about his visit to Austria in 1945.

f ☐ Bond arrests Smythe.

g ☐ Smythe shoots Bond.

CHAPTER 2

MAJOR SMYTHE TALKS TO BOND

Ten minutes passed, and now Bond was back in the room. Major Smythe was ready to tell his story:

It all started when I brought that big box of German secret police documents back to my hotel room in Kitzbühel,' he began. 'I took the documents out, and read them quickly. They were the usual things: names and addresses, a few **reports**. *Our people in Salzburg were interested in documents like those about the secret work that the Germans did during the war. They wanted to arrest war criminals, you see. Then, at the bottom of the box, I found an* **envelope**. *It had the words SECRET. OPEN ONLY IN THE GREATEST NEED in red letters on it. I opened it and found a piece of paper inside. It read, 'FRANZISKANER HALT. 100 METRES EAST UNDER ROCKS. GUN BOX. TWO* **BARS**, *24* **CARAT**. *20 KILOGRAMS EACH.'*

report what someone writes to explain what has happened

envelope a paper cover that you put a letter in

bar a long, thick, flat piece of something

carat a measure of the quality of gold; 24 carat gold is more expensive than 9 carat gold

map a picture that shows things like hills, lakes, and rivers from above

hut a little house

Major Smythe stopped for a minute, and looked at Bond before he went on:

Forty kilograms of twenty-four carat gold! That meant about forty or fifty thousand pounds in those days, and I was the only person who knew about it. I quickly burned the paper and the envelope. Then I took out my army **map** *and found Franziskaner Halt on it. It was a small* **hut**, *high up in the mountains above Kitzbühel. There were forty kilograms of gold under some rocks 100 metres from that hut. And it was only 15 kilometres, and five hours of climbing, away.*

So you're right, Mr Bond. I took a car, and I drove to Oberhauser's house at four in the morning. I arrested him, and explained that I was taking him to Munich for questioning. His family were crying. They said that he wasn't a criminal. It was still dark when we drove away.

Oberhauser was worried, of course. Many people were going to prison at that time for things that they did in the war. But we began to talk while we drove through the mountains, and things were soon friendlier. After about half an hour, the sun began to come up. At first, it was only a red light on the tops of the mountains. A really beautiful day was beginning. We spoke about the mountains, and about walking and climbing there in the days before the war. Just then, I stopped the car by some trees. 'Oberhauser,' I said. 'We've talked a lot, and I know now that you're not a criminal. I have a plan. Let's take a day's holiday, and go climbing in the mountains. At the end of the day, we'll go back to Kitzbühel. I'll tell my people there that we went to Munich, and that everything is fine. Then you can go free.'

*Oberhauser was very happy, and he agreed to the plan at once. We drove off the road and through the trees. There was a **track** going up, and we could see a hut far up on the side of the nearest mountain. 'That hut is the Franziskaner Halt,' said Oberhauser. 'We can walk up there in about five hours. There's a **glacier** up there, too. It's a very beautiful place.'*

*We got out of the car and began walking. The sun was high in the sky now, and soon it was hot. For three hours, we walked up the track. It was hard work. I walked behind Oberhauser, and I thought about what to do with him when I found the gold. I was sorry for him, but I had a gun and he didn't. And he was the enemy. Then we arrived at the foot of the glacier. From here, we had to climb a **cliff** up to the hut. Luckily I had a good guide.*

track a narrow road for people to walk along up a mountain

glacier a cold river of ice that moves very slowly

cliff a wall of rock on a mountain that you can fall down easily

At about ten o'clock, we arrived at the hut. We were now more than 3,000 metres up, and I felt tired. Oberhauser went inside the hut to light a fire. I walked to the east, and after a hundred metres, I found a pile of stones. I walked back to the hut, and called Oberhauser. I told him that I wanted to see the glacier. We climbed up the cliff to a place just above it, with Oberhauser in front of me. At the top, I took out my Webley and shot him, twice, in the back of the head. He fell down onto the glacier and lay still on the snow.

After that, I went back to the **pile** of stones, and began moving them away. They were heavy, and it was hard work. At first I found nothing, and I felt worried. Then I saw the corner of a **metal** box. I moved some bigger stones away, and saw that it was an old German Army gun box. This was good news. It had a lock on it, and I couldn't open it, but I was sure that the gold was inside. I sat down for fifteen minutes, thinking about the money and all the things that I could do with it. Then I tried to **lift** the box. It's not easy to lift forty kilos, I can tell you. In the end, I pulled it to the top of the cliff and pushed it over. The box fell, turning slowly. Then it hit the rocks at the bottom of the cliff.

Climbing down wasn't easy. I stopped first at the glacier, and went to look at Oberhauser's body. It wasn't in a very good place; anyone who climbed up to the hut could see it. I pulled it to the nearest **crevasse**, and pushed it in. I pushed some snow down on top. Then I went to look for the gun box.

pile a number of things one on top of the other

metal gold and silver are expensive metals; iron is a cheaper metal

lift to take in your arms and carry

crevasse a long, narrow hole in a glacier

READING CHECK

Put these sentences in the correct order. Number them 1–10.

a ☐ Smythe arrested Hannes Oberhauser, and took him away in a car.

b ☐ Major Smythe found a box of German papers.

c ☐ Smythe found something interesting at the bottom of the box of papers.

d ☐ Smythe found out where Franziskaner Halt was.

e ☐ Smythe found the gold.

f ☐ Smythe killed Oberhauser.

g ☐ Smythe hid Oberhauser's dead body.

h ☐ Smythe pushed the box over the cliff.

i ☐ Oberhauser and Smythe agreed to climb up to Franziskaner Halt.

j ☐ Oberhauser and Smythe arrived at Franziskaner Halt.

WORD WORK

1 Find nine more new words from Chapter 2 in the wordsquare.

S	F	T	U	U	H	H	L	J
D	X	K	R	O	U	C	C	L
Q	C	A	R	A	T	T	R	L
E	N	V	E	L	O	P	E	G
E	V	N	P	O	O	O	V	V
D	Q	U	O	C	K	B	A	R
S	S	T	R	A	C	K	K	R
C	M	E	T	A	L	K	S	Z
I	A	G	L	A	C	I	E	R
P	P	F	A	A	Y	Y	E	D

2 Use the words from Activity 1 to complete the sentences.

a A few of the papers in the box were ...report...s.

b Major Smythe found the information about the gold in an ....

c Smythe looked for Franziskaner Halt on his ....

d Smythe and Oberhauser walked up a .... into the mountains.

e Franziskaner Halt was a small .... in the mountains.

f There was a beautiful .... near Franziskaner Halt.

g Smythe pushed Oberhauser's body into a ....

h Smythe found the gold in a .... box.

i The gold was in two .... s.

j It was twenty-four .... gold.

GUESS WHAT

What does Major Smythe do in the next chapter? Tick five boxes.

a ☐ He marries an English woman.

b ☐ He loses the gold.

c ☐ He smuggles the gold into England.

d ☐ He smuggles the gold into Jamaica.

e ☐ He is arrested for smuggling the gold.

f ☐ He finds out that there is a problem with the gold.

g ☐ He sells some of the gold.

h ☐ He meets Oberhauser's wife again.

13

CHAPTER 3
WHAT HAPPENED TO THE GOLD?

Major Smythe felt old, tired, and worried.

'Can I bring you a drink?' he asked Bond.

'No. Just tell me what happened next,' Bond replied.

The major went on with his story:

*Well, I found the gun box at the bottom of the cliff. It broke open when it fell, and inside I could see two bars with brown paper around them. I pulled off the paper, and there was the gold, bright in the sun. The bars had the **mark** of the German Central Bank, and the date '1943' on them. At first, I left them in the box and began pulling it down the track. This was hard work but it was easier than carrying them. The sun was really hot now, and my face and back were burning. Of course, the track was going down the mountain, so that helped. But after some hours, I arrived at the trees, and the track didn't go down any more. I couldn't pull the box along behind me now. I had to carry the gold.*

mark a picture or letters that you put on something to show that it belongs to you; to show where something important is with a picture or letter

So I took the bars out of the box. Then I made a hole under some rocks to hide the box in. I put the rocks back very carefully. I didn't want anybody to find the box and begin to ask questions. After that, I took my shirt off and made a bag out of it to carry the bars on my back. Have you ever tried to walk with forty kilos of gold on your back? It's heavy work! And every few metres, the bars fell out of my shirt and onto my legs. That hurt, and I had to sit down and make my shirt into a bag again. This happened hundreds of times. I really don't know how I carried that gold back to the car, but I did it.

I knew that I couldn't take the gold with me. I wasn't sure where I was going next, or when I could go back to England. So I took the gold into the trees, and I put the bars under some rocks there. I marked the place where I hid them on my map. Then I drove back to my hotel and went to bed. The next day, we left Ober Aurach. Six months later, I was back in London. My army days were nearly at an end.

Major Smythe looked at Bond again. But Bond said nothing, and the major went on:

*So I was at home in England, but the gold was back in Austria. Luckily I still had friends in the Secret Service, and they found me a job in Munich for six months. One weekend I borrowed a car, drove to Kitzbühel, and brought the gold back to Munich. Then I flew to London for the weekend twice. Each time, I took a bar of gold with me in an old bag. I had to smuggle a bag with twenty kilos of gold in it onto a plane twice! Once I had the bars in England, I took all the marks off them, and I hid them in my **aunt**'s flat in West London.*

aunt your mother's (or father's) sister

A few months later, I left the army and married Mary. We both thought that life in London was cold and boring. So I took her to my aunt's flat and showed her the bars. With that gold, I explained, we could have a very good life in the sun in Jamaica. 'We're rich, Mary,' I told her. 'But it's a secret. I don't want any criminals to learn about our gold.'

*Jamaica was a wonderful country for my wife and me when we were young. The weather was good, and we soon made lots of friends. Mary played a lot of tennis, and I played **golf**. In the evenings, we met our friends for dinner in restaurants around the island.*

Now, you can't just go into a shop or a bank and sell gold bars, so at first Mary and I lived on the money that we brought with us from England. But for a year I talked very carefully to different businesspeople in Kingston. And in these conversations, I heard about the Foo brothers. They were two rich Chinese men who lived and worked in Kingston. They had business interests all over the world and, most importantly for me, in Hong Kong. This was good news for me because Macau, just a few kilometres across the sea from Hong Kong, was the centre for gold smuggling at that time.

*There were no problems during my first meeting with the Foo brothers – until they saw the gold. The Foos were worried because the bars had no marks on them. 'I'm afraid that we must look at these carefully, Major,' the older brother said. 'We must be sure that they're one hundred **per cent** gold. Can we meet again after lunch?'*

'Of course,' I said. I didn't enjoy my lunch. But when I went back to the Foos' office, the two brothers were smiling. And I saw a paper and a beautiful Parker pen on the desk.

golf a game where you hit a ball into a number of holes

per cent a hundredth part of something (%)

lead a very heavy grey metal

'We've looked at your bars, Major,' said the older Mr Foo. 'And they have an interesting story.'

'But are they real gold?' I asked.

*'They're German, Major, and they're ten per cent **lead**,' answered the older brother. 'The German Central Bank added lead to gold during the Second World War – so stupid of them.'*

'Hmm, that's interesting, Mr Foo,' I said. 'The question is - can you sell this gold?'

'Yes, Major, we can,' replied the older Foo. 'But for less than usual. What were you thinking of for the two bars?'

'Perhaps twenty thousand pounds?' I replied.

'Major, I think that we can do better than that,' said the older brother. 'Perhaps we can sell them for a hundred thousand dollars. Of course, there will be our costs, too.'

'And what are your costs?' I asked.

'Only ten per cent,' answered old Mr Foo.

I knew that ten per cent was very high. One per cent was usual. But this was still very good news. So I stood up, shook hands with both the brothers, and **signed** the paper.

After that, every three months I visited the Foo brothers, and every three months I came away with five hundred new Jamaican Pounds. The gold bars **became** smaller, centimetre by centimetre, but they were big bars, and I wasn't worried. And so the months turned into years under the hot sun. I and my wife became older and heavier. Then I began having heart problems. The doctor told me to stop smoking, and to eat more carefully. Mary tried to help me, but I felt angry at this. I didn't want her help. So, as far as I could, I stayed away from her. She became unhappier. Then, one night, she took too many sleeping pills and didn't wake up. After that, I moved away from Kingston to this house by the sea. And now I'm waiting to die here.

'Well, Mr Bond,' said Major Smythe. 'Is this the story that you wanted?'

'Yes,' said Bond.

'Do you want me to write it out and sign it?' asked the major.

'You can if you like,' replied Bond. 'But not for me. The police will want that. I'll just tell them everything, and they can decide.'

'I see,' said Major Smythe. 'Can I ask you one thing?'

'You can,' answered Bond.

'How did they find out?'

'It was a small glacier. Oberhauser's body came out at the bottom of the crevasse earlier this year. Some climbers found it. He had his papers on him. We just had to work back to 1945,' explained Bond. 'The **bullets** decided everything.'

'And why did they ask you to come here?'

'I wasn't busy,' said Bond, 'and I wanted to do it.'

'Why?' asked Major Smythe.

'Oberhauser was one of my friends. He taught me to ski before

sign to write your name on a paper to say that you agree to something

become (past **became**, **become**) to begin to be

bullet a small piece of metal that you use in a gun

the war when I was fifteen or sixteen,' answered Bond. 'He was like a father to me.'

'I see,' said Major Smythe. 'I'm sorry.'

James Bond stood up. 'I must go back to Kingston now,' he said. 'The police will come for you in about a week, I think.' He walked through the garden to his car, and drove away.

READING CHECK

Correct ten more mistakes in the story.

track

Major Smythe pulled the box of gold down the cliff. When he came to the trees, he took the gold out of the box, and carried it in a bag. He made the bag from his hat. When he arrived at his car, he hid the gold up some trees. He went back to London, but six years later he came back. He smuggled the gold back to London, and hid it in a house there. Then he married Mary, and they went to live in Jamaica. They made a lot of friends in Jamaica, and Mary played a lot of football. The major took the gold to the Foo brothers. They told him that it was French gold, but that they could sell it for him. The Foo brothers gave the major five hundred Jamaican Pounds every three months. After some years, the major started to have problems with his legs, and his doctor told him to stop smoking. Mary was more and more unhappy, and one night she took too many heart pills, and she died. Then the major left Kingston, and he moved to a house by the hospital. Oberhauser's body came out of the glacier after many years. They knew who he was because he had his guns with him.

WORD WORK

Use the words in the gold bars to complete the sentences.

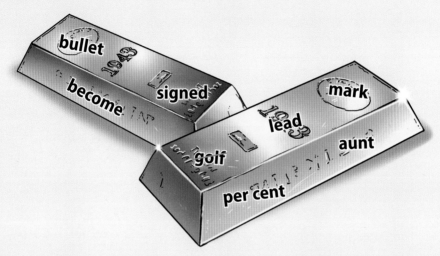

a We like to play ......golf...... at the weekend.

b This box is very heavy because it was made of ....

c The number of people in our town has gone up by ten .... in twenty years.

d He shot a .... from his gun.

e She finished the letter, and .... her name at the bottom.

f I often go to visit my .... with my mother – because they're sisters.

g If you eat too much, you'll soon .... fatter.

h My gold ring has a .... on it to show that it was made in Italy.

GUESS WHAT

What does Major Smythe do in the next chapter? Match the first and second part of each sentence.

1	He takes his mask and his spear	**a**	and spears it.
2	He finds a scorpion fish	**b**	and goes down to the sea.
3	He kills the scorpion fish	**c**	to shake Octopussy's tentacle.
4	He thinks about going to the hospital	**d**	to visit Octopussy.
5	He goes out onto the reef	**e**	but the spines hurt him.
6	He puts out his hand	**f**	but it's too far away.

CHAPTER 4
THE STORY IN THE NEWSPAPER

Major Dexter Smythe swam slowly along the reef. He thought about Bond's last words to him before he got into his car. Why wait a week? Why didn't he telephone the police immediately, and ask them to arrest him at once? Why didn't he just bring the police with him? Why did Bond give him a week to make his plans? Was he a kind man? Major Smythe didn't think so. He knew what Bond wanted. He wanted a tidy **suicide**, with no questions, and nothing about the Secret Service in the newspapers.

'What do I do?' he thought. 'Do I kill myself? Or do I fight this? It all happened during the war, and nobody really knows what happened at the Franziskaner Halt. Perhaps Oberhauser knew about the gold. Perhaps he had a gun. Perhaps he tried to shoot me before I shot him.'

Perhaps he wasn't finished after all. Major Smythe saw a picture of himself speaking to the police in London, and he looked very good in his army clothes. But it was difficult to swim and to think at the same time. So Major Smythe decided to think later. Octopussy was waiting for her lunch. Where was that scorpion fish?

He put his mask back on, and he held his spear ready. Then he swam between the rocks and the coral, looking carefully to the right and the left. He saw something dark green moving in the rocks. It was a **lobster**. Lobster makes a wonderful lunch, but today Major Smythe wasn't interested. Then, ten minutes later, he saw a brown rock that wasn't really a rock. He stopped, and put his feet down on the bottom of the sea. It was a big fish, perhaps three or four hundred grams. He watched while twelve or thirteen poison spines came up on the scorpion fish's back. Its red eyes were watching him carefully.

suicide when someone kills himself or herself

lobster an animal with ten legs and two big claws that lives near rocks in the sea; people eat it

Major Smythe knew that he had to bring his spear down onto the middle of the fish's body. The head was too hard even for his very **sharp** spear. He moved his feet up, and swam over the fish. Now! But he was too late. The fish swam suddenly up and underneath him. Major Smythe stopped and turned in the water.

The scorpion fish was back on the bottom of the sea behind him. This time he didn't miss it. The scorpion fish was on the end of his spear, ready for Octopussy.

It was hard work, and he could feel a sharp **pain** in his heart. He must be careful. Holding the spear, he walked back to the beach. He put the spear and the scorpion fish next to him, and sat down.

After about five minutes, Major Smythe began to feel something strange on his **chest**. He looked down and saw a white circle of skin, with a little blood in the centre.

'You hurt me!' he said, looking down at the scorpion fish. 'I was so careful, but you hurt me with one of your spines!'

'What happens next?' he asked himself. Then he remembered. 'The pain will become worse, and in fifteen minutes I'll be dead. There are things that doctors in a hospital can do to stop the poison. But there isn't time for that. The nearest hospital is an hour away.'

The pain was already stronger. It started at his chest, and went through his whole body. He fell to the ground, and he saw the scorpion fish in front of him.

'Octopussy!' he cried. 'It's time for your lunch.'

sharp that can cut or make holes like a knife; very strong and sudden (of pain)

pain the feeling that you have in your body when you are hurt

chest the top half of the front of the body

He put on his mask, and he pulled himself and the spear down the beach and into the water. It was fifty metres to Octopussy's home in the reef. The pain was now terrible, and Major Smythe was screaming silently into his mask.

Octopussy was at home. He could see the old brown bag and the big eye. She was watching him. It was difficult to do anything now, the pain was so bad. He held the spear, and the scorpion fish, just in front of Octopussy's hole. Three tentacles came out, feeling around the fish. Then they jumped, but not at the fish. They took Major Smythe's arm.

'We're shaking hands,' he thought. 'Wonderful.'

But the octopus wasn't shaking hands. It was pulling down strongly. More tentacles came up to help, and the pulling became harder and harder.

Major Smythe tried to pull back, but he couldn't. The scorpion fish's poison was working. Then Octopussy took his hand in her mouth, and started to eat a finger.

Two young Jamaican men were fishing from a boat when they found him. They killed the octopus with Major Smythe's spear, and they took the major's body to the police. Then they took the octopus and the scorpion fish home for dinner.

'MAN **DROWNS** ON REEF' said the story in the Jamaica Times newspaper the next morning. James Bond read the story back in London the following day. 'Suicide,' he thought. Then he wrote 'death by drowning' at the end of his report, and closed it for the last time.

drown to die in water

READING CHECK

1 Are these sentences true or false? Tick the boxes.

		True	False
a	Major Smythe thinks that James Bond wants him to kill himself.	☑	☐
b	Smythe wants to have lobster for lunch.	☐	☐
c	Smythe kills the scorpion fish with his spear.	☐	☐
d	Smythe wants to give the scorpion fish to Bond.	☐	☐
e	Octopussy takes Smythe's foot in its mouth.	☐	☐
f	Bond reads about Smythe's death in the newspaper.	☐	☐

2 Correct the mistakes in these sentences.

    Nobody

a ~~Everybody~~ knew what really happened at Franziskaner Halt.

b There are twelve or thirteen poison spines on a scorpion fish's head.

c The spines hit Smythe on the arm.

d There is a hospital near Smythe's house.

e Two men were swimming from their boat when they found Smythe on the reef.

f The two men took the octopus and the scorpion fish home for their children.

WORD WORK

Find words in the octopuses to complete the sentences.

a Don't cut yourself with that _sharp_ knife!  ahprs

b We're having _ _ _ _ _ _ _ for lunch today! Mmm!  belostr

c He hit my face, and then my _ _ _ _ _ _.  stceh

d Be careful! The river water's moving very fast. You could _ _ _ _ _ _.  dnorw

e Did someone kill her, or was it _ _ _ _ _ _ _ _?  cdeiisu

f I took some pills to stop the _ _ _ _ in my head.  ainp

GUESS WHAT

What happens to the gold after the story ends? Choose from these ideas or add your own.

a James Bond comes back to Jamaica, and takes it to a London bank.

b The Foo brothers hide it.

c It goes to Oberhauser's family in Austria.

d The Kingston police take it and sell it to pay for more police officers.

e ....

f ....

g ....

BEFORE READING

These people are in the story *The Living Daylights*. Match each sentence with a picture. Use a dictionary to help you.

1 Paul Sender

2 M

3 The cello player

4 James Bond

5 Number 272

6 'Trigger'

a ☐ This person plays in an orchestra.

b ☐ This person needs to cross from East Berlin to West Berlin.

c ☐ This person is a Russian sniper.

d ☐ This person works for the British Secret Service in Berlin.

e ☐ This person is the head of the British Secret Service in London.

f ☐ This person works for the British Secret Service. His job is to kill somebody.

THE LIVING DAYLIGHTS

CHAPTER 1

TARGET PRACTICE FOR BOND

7TH JULY 1961: 9.00 P.M.

infra-red with this light, you can see things in the dark

Sniperscope this goes on top of a gun; you look through it to see what you are going to shoot

target something that you shoot at and try to hit the middle of

wind flag a piece of cloth that shows the way that the air is moving when it's windy

aim when you move a gun carefully towards a target; to move a gun carefully towards a target

trigger you pull this part of a gun to shoot it

James Bond was beginning to feel uncomfortable. It was nine o'clock on a windy evening, and it was nearly dark. He was lying on the wet ground, and he was looking through an **infra-red Sniperscope** at a **target** 480 metres away. The target was only two metres across, and Bond could just see the ten centimetre circle in the centre. His last shot was just outside that circle, and that wasn't good. He looked again at the **wind flags**. The wind was stronger now than before, so he looked through the Sniperscope and changed his **aim**. Then he put his finger carefully back on the **trigger** and pulled it.

The shot rang out loudly across the empty fields. Bond looked at the target again. Yes, this time the hole was inside the circle, at the bottom right.

'That's better,' said a voice behind him. 'Now I want you to try five quick shots.'

Quick shooting was always difficult, even with a wonderful gun like this. And it was a very special gun, a .308 Winchester with a Sniperscope and some other important changes. It was made for a special job, and it was new to Bond. His hand was wet. He **wiped** it on the leg of his trousers, and took hold of the gun again.

'Ready?' asked the voice behind him.

'Yes,' Bond was looking through the Sniperscope.

'I'll count down from five. Five, four, three, two, one. **Fire**!'

Five shots rang out in five seconds. Bond **wiped** his eyes and looked at the target again. There were only four holes inside the circle. He put down the gun, stood up, and turned to the soldier behind him.

'Your last shot went under the target. That often happens

wipe to make something clean by moving it across something, or by moving your hand across it

fire to shoot a gun

when people shoot fast,' said the soldier.

'I know. The gun is fine. I just wanted to see what it could do,' said Bond. 'Thank you for your help. I must leave for London now.'

The **daylight** was going while the two men walked across the field to Bond's car.

'That's a nice car. I've never seen a Bentley Continental like that before. Is it a special job?' asked the soldier.

'Yes,' said Bond. 'Mulliner's did some work on it for me. It's larger inside now. I prefer that. Well, good night, and thank you again for your help.'

The Continental drove away fast down the road.

'Now why did the Ministry of Defence send him down here for target practice so late in the day?' the soldier asked himself. 'And where's he driving so quickly now? Perhaps he's on his way to meet a young woman somewhere.'

daylight the light of the day

But Bond wasn't on his way to meet a woman. He was going to the airport. He had a ticket for a special British Airways **flight** to Berlin. The gun was also going to Berlin, but on another plane, not with Bond. He was driving fast, but he wasn't thinking about the road.

He was thinking about the plane and his flight to Berlin at midnight. He looked at the clock in the car. It was ten-fifteen, but the airport was only a few kilometres away. He thought about his meeting with M at two-thirty that afternoon. And he thought about a man that he would see in Berlin. A man that he would see for only a few minutes. A man that he would kill.

7TH JULY 1961: 2.30 P.M.

When 007 walked into his office at two-thirty, M was sitting at his desk, with his back to the door. He turned around and looked at Bond. He didn't like this job, and he wanted to finish it soon.

'Good afternoon, Bond,' said M. Then he went on quickly. 'It's about Number 272. He's one of our best men. He's been in Russia for fifteen years, but he needs to get out. Now! And we need to help him. He's got some very important information for us. He's travelled across Russia and Poland, and as far as East Berlin. He's going to try and cross over to West Berlin tomorrow night, or one or two nights after that. We know where he wants to cross, and we know that it will be between six and seven in the evening.'

M stopped for a minute and looked at Bond. 'But there's a little problem, Bond. The Russians know about Number 272, and they know where he wants to cross. Their plan is to use their best **sniper** to stop him - someone that they call "Trigger" in Russian.'

'Where do I come in?' asked Bond. He knew the answer. This was dirty work. He didn't like it, and he wanted to hear M say it. But he also knew that this was his job. This was why he had two Os in front of his number seven.

flight when you fly somewhere on a plane

sniper a person with a gun who hides somewhere and shoots people from that hiding place

'Where do you come in, 007?' asked M. 'You know very well. You're the man who must kill the sniper before he kills Number 272.'

Bond stood up. 'All right,' he said. 'But I'll need a very good gun. And I'll need some **practice** with it.'

'I'm sorry, 007,' said M. 'It's not a nice job, but someone has to do it. There's a gun ready for you. You have target practice at 8.15 this evening. And there's a flight to Berlin for you at midnight.'

practice when you do something many times so that you can do it well

READING CHECK

Are these sentences true or false? Tick the boxes.

		True	False
a	James Bond always used a special .308 Winchester.	☐	☑
b	Shooting quickly is easy with a .308 Winchester.	☐	☐
c	Bond's last, quick shot with the gun is good.	☐	☐
d	Bond drives a Bentley Continental.	☐	☐
e	Number 272 has been in Russia for fifteen years.	☐	☐
f	The Russians know that Number 272 wants to cross into West Berlin.	☐	☐
g	Bond's job is to shoot Number 272.	☐	☐
h	Trigger works for the Russians.	☐	☐
i	Bond takes the .308 Winchester to Berlin with him.	☐	☐
j	Bond is happy about this job.	☐	☐

WORD WORK

Complete each sentence with a word in the gun.

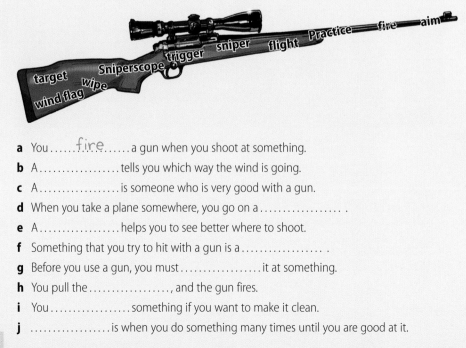

a You ......fire...... a gun when you shoot at something.

b A .... tells you which way the wind is going.

c A .... is someone who is very good with a gun.

d When you take a plane somewhere, you go on a ....

e A .... helps you to see better where to shoot.

f Something that you try to hit with a gun is a ....

g Before you use a gun, you must .... it at something.

h You pull the .... , and the gun fires.

i You .... something if you want to make it clean.

j .... is when you do something many times until you are good at it.

GUESS WHAT

What does James Bond do in the next chapter? Tick two boxes.

a ☐ He arrives in Berlin.

b ☐ He kills Trigger.

c ☐ He kills Number 272.

d ☐ He goes to Russia.

e ☐ He sees a beautiful woman.

f ☐ He loses his gun.

g ☐ He goes back to London.

CHAPTER 2
THE BORDER WITH EAST BERLIN

bombed hit by things that fall from a plane, killing people and breaking buildings

border where two countries, or two parts of a country, meet

Kochstrasse /ˈkɒxʃtraːsə/

Wilhelmstrasse /ˈvɪlhelmʃtraːsə/

weed a wild plant in a city

bell you ring this to ask someone to open their front door

lift this takes people to different floors in a building

Berlin was **bombed** over three hundred times between 1940 and 1945. There were not many buildings near the **border** between East and West Berlin, and the tall building on the corner of **Kochstrasse** and **Wilhelmstrasse** stood alone. Bond paid the taxi driver and looked around. He saw bombed walls, tall **weeds**, and bright yellow lights. He walked over to the front door, and pushed the **bell** for the fourth floor flat. The door opened immediately, and he walked in.

It was dark inside the building. Bond could smell old cigarettes and yesterday's dinner – the smell of hundreds of buildings all over Europe. He went up to the fourth floor in an old, tired, **lift**.

Number Two in Berlin, Paul Sender, was a tall, boring, man in his forties. Bond was unhappy before he met Sender. After five minutes with him, he did not feel any happier.

The flat had a bedroom, a bathroom, and a kitchen. In the bedroom, one of the two beds was next to the window.

'Do you want to look out?' asked Sender, turning off the light.

'Lie on the bed, and put your head under the **curtains**,' he went on. 'I don't want to open them because perhaps the Russians are watching. Look to the left.'

Bond lay on the bed. He put his head through the curtains, and looked out. Today he was not looking at a target, but across 200 metres of bombed buildings and weeds. He could see a street in the middle of it all.

'That street is Zimmerstrasse – the border with East Berlin,' said Sender. 'It's the best place to cross, as you can see. There are empty buildings, old walls, and **thick** weeds on each side. But in the middle there are thirty metres across the street. The lights are bright, and the Russians will want to kill him there. '

'Yes,' said Bond, quietly.

'Now, look at that tall, modern building on the left. We're watching it carefully. Most of the lights are on all night. Trigger isn't going to fire from a room where the lights are on. But there are four windows on the corner. You can see the street very well from them, and they're always dark. Those windows are 300 metres from here.'

curtain people close this in front of a window to stop people looking in

thick growing near together, making it difficult to see between them

Bond lay in bed. He listened to Sender who was asleep in the other bed. Bond was thinking about the office building across the border, and its four dark windows.

Bond woke up in the middle of the day. The flat was empty. He looked out of the window. He could see everything better in the daylight: the 300 metres between his window and Trigger's windows, the bombed walls, the weeds. He found some food in the kitchen. There was a note on the bread:

> Go out if you want, but be back by 17.00. Everything will be ready for you.

Bond burned the note, then cooked himself some breakfast. After breakfast, he took the lift downstairs, and went out. He walked for two hours in the trees of the Grunewald. Then he had a late lunch, and visited a book shop on his way back to the flat. In the street outside, Bond walked past an old black Opel. A man had his head inside it, and there were strange noises coming from the **engine**.

Sender was in the apartment when Bond arrived, and he explained. The man with the car was a 'friend'. Sender could talk to him by **walkie-talkie**. When Bond began to shoot, he would make some very loud noises with the car to hide the sound of the shots.

'We don't want people to call the police!' explained Sender.

Bond thought that the car was a good plan, and he was even happier when he looked into the bedroom. His gun was on the bed, and the end of it was **pointing** out of the window. The metal of the gun and the Sniperscope were black, and there were black clothes and hats for Bond and Sender, too.

'Do you want to eat something? Or have a cup of tea perhaps?' asked Sender.

'No, thanks,' said Bond. 'I'll read while I'm waiting. I've just bought myself a book.' He lay down on the bed, by the gun, and

engine the machine in a car that makes it move

walkie-talkie a small radio that you can use to talk with another person not very far way

point to be turned one way

took out his book – a German detective story. The time went past quickly until suddenly Sender spoke.

'It's five-thirty. Are you ready?'

He turned off the lights. Bond put on his black hat and clothes and lay on the bed, his head under the curtains. Through the Sniperscope, he watched people coming out of the building three hundred metres away. The four windows on the corner were dark and open at the bottom. Bond couldn't really see inside the rooms, but nothing was moving.

Suddenly Bond saw a group of twenty young women who were walking over to the building. They were carrying **musical instruments** in black **cases**, and talking and laughing together. It was a women's **orchestra**. It was surprising to see lots of happy people in that unhappy place. One woman, taller than the others, caught Bond's eye. She had long hair, and was carrying a **cello**. In the wind, everything about her was flying: the gold of her hair, her skirt, her coat. Bond watched her carefully through the Sniperscope while she laughed with the two girls next to her. Then they all went through the door and into the building.

'See that orchestra?' asked Sender. 'They're there every night. They'll play in a minute. They're not bad.'

Bond said nothing. He watched the door of the building. It was 5.50. Still ten minutes. When would Trigger arrive?

musical instrument you make music with this; a guitar is a musical instrument

case a big, hard bag

orchestra a number of players of different musical instruments who make music together

cello a big, wooden musical instrument with strings; you stand it between your legs to play it

READING CHECK

Correct 10 more mistakes in the story.

taxi

James Bond takes a ~~bus~~ to the flat in Wilhelmstrasse, and he rings the bell for the fourth floor flat. He goes up to the flat, and meets Paul Sender, Number One in Berlin. In the bedroom, one of the two beds is next to the door.

Bond looks out of the window, and from there, he can see over into West Berlin. There is a tall, modern building on the left. In the building, there are two windows which are always dark, and they think that Trigger is in one of those rooms.

The next day, Bond gets up early, and has breakfast. Then he goes out for a walk, and buys a newspaper. When he comes back to the flat, he sees an old black bus in the street outside. At 5.30, they turn on the lights, and Bond lies on the bed with his gun. He sees forty young women in the street. They are going to play music in the tall, modern building. Bond is very interested in one of them – a tall woman with dark hair.

WORD WORK

1 Find eleven more new words from Chapter 2 in the wordsquare.

B	O	R	D	E	R	T	T	C
O	R	W	W	E	E	D	D	A
M	C	U	R	T	A	I	N	S
B	H	Z	X	T	N	C	B	E
E	E	N	G	I	N	E	E	E
D	S	L	I	F	T	L	L	Q
D	T	H	I	C	K	L	L	L
L	R	H	H	K	K	O	J	S
Q	A	P	O	I	N	T	B	X

2 Use the words from Activity 1 in the correct form to complete the sentences.

a When you arrive at someone's front door, you often ring the ...... bell ....

b When you want to carry a musical instrument, you can put it in a ....

c A car needs an .... to move.

d A number of people playing music together is an ....

e Many cities in Europe were badly .... between 1939 and 1945.

f I like listening to the .... It's a beautiful musical instrument.

g The .... between East and West Berlin was very difficult to cross in the 1970s.

h Sender .... out of the window to show Bond where 272 will try to cross from the other side.

i There are a lot of .... growing in the gardens of the empty houses.

j The old city walls are very ....

k She opened the .... , and looked out of the window.

l I went up to the fourth floor in the ....

GUESS WHAT

What happens in the next chapter? Tick the boxes.

1 Number 272…
  a tries to cross the border and is killed. ☐
  b doesn't try to cross the border. ☐
  c crosses the border safely. ☐

2 James Bond…
  a shoots Trigger. ☐
  b sees Trigger shoot Number 272. ☐
  c doesn't see Trigger. ☐

3 Trigger…
  a shoots Number 272. ☐
  b doesn't shoot anybody. ☐
  c shoots James Bond. ☐

41

CHAPTER 3
FINGER ON THE TRIGGER

Lying on the bed inside the flat, Bond heard the sound of the women's orchestra. They were three hundred metres away, and they were **preparing** to play. Then suddenly he could hear the music.

prepare to make yourself ready

'They're playing a piece by Borodin,' said Sender. 'Russian music.'

Bond listened, and he thought about the beautiful cellist, her hands moving quickly over her cello.

'It's nearly six. Time for Number 272 to cross,' said Sender. 'Hey, what's that? Look at the bottom window on the right!'

Bond moved his Sniperscope up to the window and looked through it. Something was moving inside one of the windows on the corner of the building opposite. Then, suddenly, he could see the end of a gun at the bottom of the window. It moved around for a few seconds, and then stopped. It was pointing at Zimmerstrasse.

'Can you see it well? What **kind** of gun is it?' asked Sender. He was excited.

Bond looked carefully through his Sniperscope. 'It's a Kalashnikov,' he said. 'AK-47. The best gun for this job. They need to hit a running man between all those walls and weeds. But it's a surprise – because Kalashnikovs are very noisy. They're not the best kind of guns to use in the centre of a city. The enemy really want to kill Number 272.'

Bond thought for a minute, and then spoke to Sender again.

'Kalashnikovs fire quickly, so I can't wait for Trigger to shoot. I must shoot as soon as we see Number 272 – before Trigger can start to fire. Can you watch Zimmerstrasse and tell me when you see 272? I must watch Trigger.'

Bond couldn't see Trigger, he could only see the Kalashnikov. So Bond's Winchester was pointing just behind the enemy gun, into the dark room, at Trigger's body. It wasn't possible to aim at his head. It was too far away for that. It wasn't hot, but Bond was **sweating**. His face and eyes were wet, but that wasn't important. The finger on the trigger must be dry, so he wiped his hand on his trousers.

kind a type of thing; a Kalashnikov is a kind of gun

sweat to get water on your body because you are hot or worried; water that comes from your body because you are hot or worried

The minutes passed very slowly. Sometimes Bond changed his **position** to stay comfortable. The orchestra was playing, and Bond listened. How old was she? Perhaps twenty-two or twenty-three? Why does a beautiful woman decide to play the cello? A woman doesn't look very nice when she's holding a cello between her legs. Why not play something different?

'It's seven o'clock,' said Sender. 'There's nothing moving on the other side. I can see two men on this side. They're our men, and they're waiting to meet 272. But let's go on watching until Trigger leaves.'

'All right.'

It was 7.30 when the Kalashnikov went back into the dark room. One after the other, the four windows closed. Number 272 was still hiding somewhere in East Berlin. Two more nights to go!

Bond carefully moved back past the curtains,and got off the bed. He went to the bathroom, took off his black clothes, and had a long, hot shower. He went back into the bedroom, and sat down. He listened to the orchestra until eight o'clock, when it stopped. Sender was busy writing notes.

'I'm just going to look through the window another time,' said Bond. 'I want to see that beautiful cellist again.'

'I didn't see her,' said Sender. He got up, and went into the kitchen to make some tea.

Bond took the Sniperscope in his hand, and looked through it at the front door of the building on the other side of Zimmerstrasse. There was the orchestra – not so happy now. They were **probably** tired.

The tall young woman was carrying her cello case. Her hair was still beautiful in the wind. Bond watched her while she walked down Wilhelmstrasse into the dark night. Where was she going? Home to a flat somewhere? Did she have a family? Was she married? Did she have a lover?

It wasn't important. She wasn't for him.

The next day and the next evening were just the same. For a minute or two Bond saw the beautiful cellist again, arriving and leaving, through his Sniperscope. But most of the time he was waiting, waiting with his finger on the trigger, and sweat on his face and body.

On the third day, Bond wanted to stay very busy. Tonight was the last night, and he didn't want to think about it. He visited different **museums**, went to see a film, and took a long walk. He was thinking about the cello player. He was also thinking about the four dark windows, and the man that they called Trigger. Bond was preparing himself to kill the sniper that night.

probably nearly 100% sure

museum a building where people go to look at old things

READING CHECK

Are these sentences true or false? Tick the boxes.

		True	False
a	The orchestra plays German music.	☐	☑
b	Bond and Sender see a gun in the window.	☐	☐
c	Trigger has a Kalashnikov.	☐	☐
d	Bond watches Zimmerstrasse.	☐	☐
e	Sender watches Trigger.	☐	☐
f	While he is waiting for Number 272, Bond thinks about the beautiful cello player.	☐	☐
g	Trigger leaves the window at 8.30 at night.	☐	☐
h	Bond sees the orchestra walk down Zimmerstrasse.	☐	☐
i	The second day is the same as the first day.	☐	☐
j	On the third day, Bond stays in the flat.	☐	☐
k	On the third day, Bond thinks about Trigger.	☐	☐

WORD WORK

Correct the boxed mistakes in these sentences with new words from Chapter 3.

a Trigger will problem try to kill Number 272. ...probably...

b Bond's hand was wet because he was swimming a lot. ....

c A Kalashnikov was the right king of gun for Trigger. ....

d There are interesting musicians to visit in Berlin. ....

e Number 272 was preferring to cross into West Berlin. ....

f It's difficult when you don't change your postman for a long time. ....

GUESS WHAT

What happens in the next chapter? Tick two boxes.

a ☐ Trigger shoots Bond.

b ☐ Trigger shoots Sender.

c ☐ Bond shoots Trigger.

d ☐ Trigger shoots Number 272.

e ☐ Sender is angry with Bond.

f ☐ M is angry with Bond.

g ☐ Bond meets the beautiful cellist from the orchestra.

h ☐ Bond meets Number 272.

CHAPTER 4
CROSSING OVER

Bond stayed in the city all day. After a very late lunch, he arrived back at the flat at five. Sender was waiting for him, and he was very **nervous**.

'Bond, where have you been? It's nearly time,' he said, importantly.

'Don't worry,' said Bond. 'I'll be fine. I've got to kill someone tonight. Me, not you. Do you think that I like that kind of work? Do you want to do it? Or are you happier with your nice comfortable office job? If you want to make trouble for me, you can talk to Head Office later, after the shooting. But not now. Not just before a job like this.'

Sender said nothing, but he went into the kitchen and made tea, noisily. Bond sat down with his detective book.

Half an hour later, they were in their positions at their windows. They were lying on the beds wearing their black hats and clothes, and with their heads under the curtains. Bond had his Sniperscope and his Winchester ready. He was already sweating.

nervous a little afraid

At five past six, Sender started speaking excitedly. 'Bond, there's someone moving over there. It's 272. Wait a minute. He's stopped. No, he's moving again. There's an old wall behind him, so for now he's OK. The enemy can't see him there. But there are thick weeds in front of him now. He's coming through the weeds and they're moving. Will the Russians think that the wind's moving them? He's through the weeds now, and he's lying face down on the ground. What's Trigger doing?' 'Nothing. Go on talking. How far is it to the border?' asked Bond.

'Fifty metres,' Sender's voice was high and nervous. 'There are some weeds, but there's a lot of open ground, too. And a wall. Number 272 must climb over that. They'll see him then, if they don't see him before. He's done another ten metres. And another. They're sure to see him now.'

Bond was sweating a lot. He wiped his hands on his trousers and put his finger back on the trigger. He was ready.

'There's something moving in the room behind the gun,' he told Sender. 'They've seen Number 272. Start the noise from the Opel!'

Sender spoke one word into the walkie-talkie. Down in the street there was a terrible noise while the car engine started up, noisily.

Bond looked again into the dark room in the building opposite him. Someone was moving there. He saw a hand come out, under the gun. Trigger was preparing to shoot.

'Now!' shouted Sender. 'He's run for the wall. He's up on it. He's going to jump!'

And then, in the Sniperscope, Bond saw a face, an eye, and beautiful gold hair lying along the top of the gun. If he fired, she was dead. Bond quickly changed his aim. His target was now the Kalashnikov, not the person behind it. He saw a yellow **flame** at the end of the Kalashnikov, and he pulled the trigger.

One of Bond's shots hit the gun, and another probably hit her hand or her arm. The Kalashnikov turned wildly under the rain of bullets, and it fell out of the window and down into the street.

'He's over!' shouted Sender. 'He's over! He's done it!'

'Get down!' shouted Bond. He jumped off the bed onto the floor while someone turned on a **searchlight** in one of the four windows across the border. The light moved quickly onto his own window. Then the guns sang out, and bullets began flying into the room, hitting the window, the curtains, and the walls. Behind the shooting, Bond heard the Opel drive off quickly down the road, and the orchestra playing. Of course! The orchestra and the Opel did the same job – to make a loud noise. The orchestra was probably louder than a Kalashnikov. And the cello case was an easy way to carry a big gun. Did the other women in the orchestra work for the enemy? Did some of their cases have guns and not musical instruments inside them? And what about the beautiful cellist? She was hurt badly, he was sure of that, probably with a bullet deep in her left arm. But he could never know. And he was sure that he would never see her again.

A last shot hit the window next to Bond, and some hot lead from the bullet fell on Bond's hand and hurt it. Then someone turned the searchlight off. Everything became suddenly dark and quiet, but Bond's ears were still singing.

flame the light that you see when something is on fire

searchlight a strong light on a building that people use to look for people in the open around it

51

After a few minutes, Sender and Bond stood up. There were pieces of glass all over their clothes and all over the floor. They went into the kitchen, closing the bedroom door behind them. The kitchen was at the back of the building, so they could turn on the light.

'Are you all right?' asked Bond.

'Yes. You?'

'Some hot lead from a bullet hurt my hand. I'll just put a **plaster** on it.'

Bond went into the bathroom, found a plaster, and put it on his hand. When he came back into the kitchen, Sender was sitting at the table and talking into the walkie-talkie. 'That's all for now. Good news about 272. Send the car quickly please. We want to leave as soon as possible. And 007 needs to give you his side of the story.'

Sender turned to Bond. 'Head Office want to know why you didn't kill the sniper. I had to tell them that I saw you change your aim at the last second. It meant that Trigger fired three or four shots. They hit the wall just behind 272. He's very lucky to be alive.'

'Trigger was a woman,' said Bond.

'A lot of the Russian snipers are women,' said Sender. 'I went to the last world shooting **competition** in Moscow. The Russians came first, second, and third in it. The two best women in the competition were Donskaya and Lomova. Perhaps Trigger is one of them. What did she look like?'

'She was the cello player in the orchestra. The tall woman with long hair,' said Bond.

'Oh, I understand,' said Sender, slowly. 'The woman that you liked.'

'That's right.'

'I'm sorry, Bond, but I had to tell Head Office about it,' said Sender. 'You didn't follow your **orders**. They told you to kill Trigger.'

'Tell them what you like,' answered Bond. 'I don't enjoy killing people.'

plaster you put this cover over a cut or other small hurt on your body

competition a game that people try to win

order when you tell somebody to do something

Outside in the street, a car drove up to the flats. It stopped in front of their building, and the bell rang twice.

'That's our car,' said Sender, standing up. 'I'm sorry, Bond, but orders are orders.'

Bond didn't really want to leave the flat now. He wanted to stay there for some time longer, and remember the beautiful girl with the cello.

He was in trouble, he knew, but she was in much deeper trouble. The Russians really wanted to kill Number 272, and they would be angry about his escape. Trigger would have some painful weeks in hospital, and some difficult questions to answer. But she was alive, he was sure of that. 'OK,' said Bond, following Sender to the door. 'Perhaps they'll take away my 00 number and give me work behind a desk. But you can tell Head Office not to worry. Poor Trigger will never be a sniper again. She's probably lost her left hand. And I'm sure that she won't want to do that kind of work in the future. She'll be too afraid. I **scared the living daylights out of** her. That's not bad for a night's work, is it? Let's go.'

scare the living daylights out of to make someone feel very afraid

READING CHECK

Put these sentences in the correct order. Number them 1–10.

a ☐ Bond and Sender go back into the kitchen.

b ☐ Bond leaves the flat.

c ☐ Bond sees Trigger's long, gold hair.

d ☐ Bond shoots Trigger.

e ☐ Bond comes back to the flat at five o'clock.

f ☐ Number 272 crosses the border.

g ☐ Number 272 starts to move nearer the border.

h ☐ Sender makes tea.

i ☐ Hot lead hurts Bond's hand.

j ☐ They start the engine of the Opel.

Trigger would have some painful weeks in hospital

WORD WORK

Complete the sentences about the story with new words from Chapter 4.

a It was dangerous to move because there was a s e͟a͟r͟c͟h͟l͟i͟g͟h͟t͟ on the building.

b Sender had to tell Head Office that Bond didn't follow o _ _ _ _ s and kill Trigger.

c Sender was very n _ _ _ _ _ _ on the third evening.

d Russian women are very successful in shooting c _ _ _ _ _ _ _ _ _ _ s.

e Bond could see the f _ _ _ _ from the Kalashnikov when Trigger fired it.

f Bond hurt his hand, so he put a p _ _ _ _ _ _ on it.

g Bond wanted to s _ _ _ _ t _ _ l _ _ _ _ _ d _ _ _ _ _ _ _ _ out of Trigger.

GUESS WHAT

What do you think happens after the end of the story? Choose from these ideas, and add your own.

a ☐ M takes away Bond's 00 number.

b ☐ Bond stays in Berlin to work with Sender.

c ☐ Trigger comes to West Berlin and meets Bond.

d ☐ Sender goes to London and gets a 00 number.

e ☐ Bond goes to Russia and meets Trigger.

f ☐ ....

g ☐ ....

h ☐ ....

Project A *Describing a character*

1 **Read the short description of James Bond, and circle the correct words. Use a dictionary to help you.**

James Bond is a **a)** *short / tall* man in his **b)** *forties / sixties*. He has **c)** *dark / fair* hair and **d)** *brown / blue* eyes. He is **e)** *handsome / ugly*, and he wears **f)** *casual / smart* clothes. He was in the Navy, but now he is a **g)** *secret agent / cellist* with the British Secret Service. He is good at **h)** *driving / selling* fast cars. He's a very **i)** *fit / unfit* man. He lives in a flat in **j)** *Moscow / London* and speaks English and German. He often visits the Austrian Alps to **k)** *play golf / ski* there.

2 Which phrases in the box describe Major Smythe, Mr Foo, and Trigger? Write them in the correct part of the table below. Use a dictionary to help you.

in *his / her twenties / forties / fifties*

has *black / grey / blonde* hair

is *fat and unfit / thin / slim and fit*

wears *smart / elegant / casual* clothes

is *a businessman / retired / a sniper*

likes *shooting / importing things / relaxing*

plays *golf / the cello / Mahjong*

lives *in East Berlin / by the beach / with brother in Kingston*

often visits *Hong Kong / parents in Moscow / the coral reef*

speaks *English / Cantonese / Russian / German*

Characters		
Major Smythe	Mr Foo	Trigger

Useful words and phrases

3 Choose one of the characters in Activity 2. Write a short description of him or her. Use the phrases you collected and the description of Bond on page 56 to help you.

Project B *Different decades*

1 **Read about Britain in the 1960s. Complete the table on page 59 with key facts. Use a dictionary to help you.**

Britain **IN THE** 1960s

The population of Britain in 1961 was about 50 million. There were only 5 million cars on British roads then. Many people still travelled by bus or train. More people started travelling by plane as air tickets became cheaper.

The Mini was a popular small, inexpensive car in the 1960s. People used the new word 'mini' for other things, too.

During the 1960s, London became an important fashion centre. The first miniskirt was sold in London in 1964. Men and women wore bright, colourful clothes, sometimes with 'flower power' designs. Women wore their hair up in 'beehive' hairstyles. Men wore their hair long!

Britain became famous for its pop music in the 1960s, too. The Beatles started singing together in 1960. Their most successful song was *She Loves You* (1963). Other bands like The Rolling Stones also began in the 1960s.

Many people watched TV in Britain in the '60s. Most ordinary British households had black-and-white TVs. Films at the cinema were in colour. *Dr No* (1962) was the first James Bond film. It starred British actor Sean Connery as Bond. British film star Julie Andrews appeared in different musical films like *The Sound of Music* (1965).

BRITAIN IN THE 1960s — KEY FACTS

Population	
Transport	
Clothes and Fashion	
Hairstyles	
Music	
Radio, Films, and TV	

2 **Complete the text about Britain in the 1940s on page 60 with the information in this table. Use a dictionary to help you.**

BRITAIN IN THE 1940s — KEY FACTS

Population	46 million
Transport	number of cars – 1 million 1st Land Rover 1948 1st passenger jet plane 1949 (de Havilland 'Comet')
Clothes and Fashion	plain, dark colours hats were worn outside
Hairstyles	**Men** – very short at back and sides **Women** – shoulder-length, with curls or waves
Music	**Most popular singer** – Vera Lynn **Most popular song** – *The White Cliffs of Dover* – Vera Lynn (1942) **Popular male singer** – George Formby
Radio, Films, and TV	Many people listened to radio, or went to cinema. Many black-and-white films. **Famous film** – Laurence Olivier's *Henry V* (1944) – in colour **Famous film star** – Vivien Leigh

The population of Britain in 1941 was about.................. .
There were only about.................. cars on the roads.
Most people travelled by bus, tram, or train. One of the new
cars of the 1940s was the.................., which was first
made in.................. . Rich people began to travel by air.
The first.................. – the 'Comet' – was made in 1949
by the British.................. company.

Clothes were mostly.................., and in..................
colours. Both men and women wore.................. when
they were outside. Men had '..................-back-and-sides'
haircuts, and women had..................-length hair, with
.... or.................. in it.

One of the most popular British singers in the 1940s
was.................., and her most popular song was
.... (1942). A popular male singer in Britain in
the '40s was.................. .

In the 1940s, many British people listened to the
.... at home, and went to see films at the
.... Many films were still black-and-white.

Laurence Olivier's colour film of Shakespeare's
.... was a famous British film of..................,
and Olivier's wife.................. was a famous British film
star of the time.

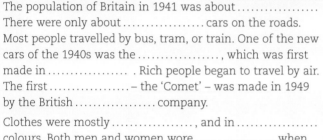

3 Research a decade in the history of your country, or another decade in the history of Britain. Write a paragraph about it. Use the texts in activities 1 and 2 to help you.

the 1910s   the 1950s   the 1990s

THE 1930s   the 1970s

GRAMMAR CHECK

Prepositions of time: *after, at, before, during*

We use after when we are describing something which happened later.

I'm very interested in your work in Austria after the end of the Second World War.

We use during when we are describing something which happened at the same time.

The German Central Bank added lead to gold during the Second World War. (= in)

We use before when we are describing something which happened earlier.

He taught me to ski before the war.

We use at with times. We also say at the weekend, at night, and at midnight.

I drove to Oberhauser's house at four in the morning

1 **Complete the police report about Hannes Oberhauser using *after*, *at*, *before*, and *during*.**

Some climbers telephoned the police in Kitzbühel **a)** ....at........ 7 o'clock on July 27th. They were going home in the evening **b)** .... climbing to the Franziskaner Halt. They telephoned from the village of Ober Aurach. They said that there was a body at the bottom of the glacier. People sometimes find things at the bottom of the glacier **c)** .... the summer — because it's hot and the snow turns to water.

We went to the glacier immediately, but we couldn't find anything **d)** .... night. We found the body **e)** .... 8.15 the next morning, **f)** .... looking for an hour. It was a man, and his papers told us that his name was Hannes Oberhauser. We talked to his family, and the last time that they saw him was in August 1945, just **g)** .... the end of the Second World War. They told us that a British soldier came to the house **h)** .... 4 o'clock in the morning, **i)** .... the sun came up, and arrested Mr Oberhauser because he said that he was a criminal **j)** .... the war. Mr Oberhauser wasn't a criminal. **k)** .... the war, in the 1930s, he worked as a skiing teacher. It was difficult for him to get work as a teacher **l)** .... the war, and so he worked on his family's farm then.

There was a bullet in the back of Mr Oberhauser's head. It was from a Webley & Scott .45. That is a British gun, so we are talking to the British police.

GRAMMAR CHECK

Comparatives and superlatives

We make comparative and superlative forms with −er and −est for short adjectives, and **more** and **most** for longer adjectives.

near > nearer, nearest   interesting > more interesting, most interesting

With short adjectives ending in consonant + y, we change the y to −ier / −iest.

angry > angrier, angriest

Good and *bad* have irregular comparatives and superlatives

good > better, best   bad > worse, worst

We usually use comparative forms of adjectives when we are comparing two things.

The older brother spoke.   Coral is more beautiful than rock.

We use superlative forms to compare one thing with a number of similar things.

He was the best mountain guide in Kitzbühel.

The hut was far up on the side of the nearest mountain.

2 Complete the sentences with the correct comparative or superlative form of the underlined adjective.

a There are a number of <u>big</u> islands in the Caribbean Sea. Cuba is the …*biggest*… of these.

b There are no hospitals <u>near</u> here. The ……………… hospital is an hour away.

c The walk to the cliff was <u>difficult</u>. The climb up the cliff was ……………… .

d Kreuzjoch, near Kitzbühel, is a <u>high</u> mountain at 2,558 metres, but Grossglockner, at 3,798 metres, is the ……………… mountain in Austria.

e Major Dexter was <u>happy</u> when he found the gold. He was ……………… when he took it to his new home in Jamaica.

f The pain in Major Smythe's chest was <u>bad</u>, but soon it became ……………… .

g There are some <u>beautiful</u> places near Kitzbühel. But I think that Franziskaner Halt is the ……………… of all of them.

h London is a <u>cold</u> place in winter, but Moscow is ……………… .

i Octopus is a <u>good</u> lunch, but lobster is a ……………… lunch.

j Stealing gold is a <u>bad</u> crime. Killing somebody is a ……………… crime.

k Major Smythe went swimming <u>early</u> in the day, but his conversation with Bond was ……………… .

GRAMMAR

GRAMMAR CHECK

Present Perfect and Past Simple

We use the Present Perfect for:

  things that happened at an indefinite time in the past

  We've looked at your bars, Major. (= we don't know when)

  experiences in our lives (often with ever)

  Have you ever tried to walk with forty kilos of gold on your back?

  things that began in the past and continue up to the present (often with for or since)

  I haven't worked for a long time.

We use the Past Simple for finished past actions.

One weekend, I borrowed a car, drove to Kitzbühel, and brought the gold back to Munich.

3 **Complete the text about Oberhauser and Bond with the verbs in brackets. Use Present Perfect or Past Simple.**

Bond and Oberhauser **a)** ......met...... (meet) in Austria in 1936. Oberhauser **b)** .... (live) all his life in Austria, but Bond **c)** .... (live) in many different countries. Oberhauser **d)** .... (not visit) Britain, but he **e)** .... (speak) good English. Oberhauser **f)** .... (work) as a mountain guide. Bond **g)** .... (not work) as a mountain guide. He **h)** .... (work) for the Secret Service for many years, and he still works for them. Oberhauser **i)** .... (teach) Bond to ski when he was a boy, and Bond **j)** .... (ski) many times since then. During his life, Oberhauser **k)** .... (climb) some of the highest mountains in Austria. Bond **l)** .... (climb) one or two mountains, but he **m)** .... (not climb) very many.

DEAD

ALIVE

GRAMMAR CHECK

Relative pronouns

We use relative pronouns (who, which, and that) to join two sentences. We often use relative pronouns to define which person or thing we are talking about. In a defining relative sentence, we can use that instead of which or who.

He was a British man. He spoke German. → *He was a British man who / that spoke German.*

He saw a rock. The rock wasn't really a rock. → *He saw a rock which / that wasn't really a rock.*

4 Rewrite these sentences changing *that* to *who* or *which*.

a Major Smythe was a British soldier that worked in Austria in 1945.

.. Major Smythe was a British soldier who worked in Austria in 1945. .

b He found an envelope that was at the bottom of a box.

....

c Franziskaner Halt was a hut that was high in the mountains.

....

d Hannes Oberhauser was a man that knew the mountains well.

....

e James Bond was the man that visited Major Smythe in Jamaica.

....

f The scorpion fish is a fish that has poison spines on its back.

....

5 Match the first and second part of these sentences. Complete each sentence with the correct relative pronoun.

a The octopus is an animal .. that / which lives in coral reefs. ....

b Major Smythe is the person ....

c The Foo brothers are the men ....

d Kitzbühel is a town in Austria ....

e James Bond is a man ....

f Poison and a bad heart are the things ....

1 He works for the Secret Service.   **4** They killed Major Smythe.

2 They bought Major Smythe's gold.   **5** It's famous for skiing.

~~**3** it lives in coral reefs.~~   **6** He killed Hannes Oberhauser.

GRAMMAR CHECK

Past Continuous

We use the Past Continuous for an action that continues for a short time in the past. We often use it in past descriptions.

Bond was driving, but he wasn't thinking about the road. He was thinking his flight to Berlin.

Twenty women were walking to the building. They were carrying musical instruments in cases.

6 Use the verbs in the box in the Past Continuous to complete this description of the night when 272 crosses the border.

aim	hold	~~lie~~	listen	look	move	play	stand	think	wait

Bond and Sender **a)** ...were lying... on the beds in the flat in Berlin. They **b)** .... out of the window. Bond **c)** .... his gun with his finger on the trigger. In the street, a man **d)** .... with his head inside an old black Opel. Near the border in East Berlin, some young women **e)** .... music, and Bond and Sender **f)** .... to them. Somewhere in East Berlin, Number 272 **g)** .... to escape. He **h)** .... about his fifteen years of work for the British Secret Service in Russia, and he **i)** .... nearer to the border with the West. Trigger was at the window of the building, and the Russian sniper **j)** .... a Kalashnikov carefully at the border.

GRAMMAR CHECK

Conditional sentences

Conditional sentences with *if* are about what will happen when we do something. For really possible things, the verb after *if* is in the Present Simple.

If I fire at Trigger, she's dead. *You can talk to Head Office if you want to.*

When the *if* part of the conditional sentence comes first, we put a comma after it.

7 **Match the first and second parts of these sentences, and complete each sentence with *if*. (Sometimes *if* begins the sentence, and sometimes it is in the middle.)**

a It's difficult to hit a target

........It's difficult to hit a target if you shoot fast.........

b You can see the target better

....

c You want to shoot someone at 500 metres

....

d You want to look out of the window

....

e Trigger can see Bond's window

....

f Number 272 is very careful

....

1 You need a very good gun   **4** He can cross the border

2 You use a Sniperscope   **5** ~~You shoot fast~~

3 She looks out of her window   **6** You must do it carefully

8 **Bond watches the women's orchestra from his window. Use the verbs in the box in the correct form to complete what he is thinking.**

> be   do   has   ~~play~~   live

There's the women's orchestra. I can listen to them again if they **a**) ......play...... tonight. That cellist is beautiful. Is she from Berlin? If she **b**) .... here, perhaps I can see her again. But if she **c**) .... Russian, she's probably leaving soon. Has she got a boyfriend? If she **d**) .... , that's bad for me. I'll probably never see her again. I'll be lucky if I **e**) .... !

GRAMMAR CHECK

Gerunds

We make the gerund by adding –ing to the verb. A gerund can be the subject or the object of a sentence.

Quick shooting was difficult, even with a wonderful gun.

You can talk to Head Office after the shooting.

We can also use a gerund after the verbs go on, like and start.

Let's go on watching until Trigger leaves.

At five past six, Sender started speaking excitedly.

We can also begin a sentence with a gerund clause.

Lying on his bed, Bond heard the sound of the women's orchestra.

9 Complete the sentences with the gerund form of the verbs in the box.

> cross   hear   kill   move   play   shoot   sit   visit   ~~wait~~   wait

a While ...*waiting*... for Number 272, Bond listened to the women's orchestra.

b When she saw Number 272, Trigger started . . . .

c Number 272 heard the shots, and stopped . . . . for a while.

d After . . . . the border, Number 272 flew to London.

e Bond doesn't like . . . . people, but it's his job.

f The worst part of Bond's '00' job was the . . . . He often waited hours to kill someone.

g . . . . a noise, Trigger looked out of the window and saw Number 272

h . . . . in his office with his back to the door, M waited for Bond to arrive.

i The orchestra finished their . . . . , and put their musical instruments away.

j Bond spent the afternoon . . . . museums.

DOMINOES Your Choice

Read *Dominoes* for pleasure, or to develop language skills. It's your choice.

Each *Domino* reader includes:
- a good story to enjoy
- integrated activities to develop reading skills and increase vocabulary
- task-based projects – perfect for CEFR portfolios
- contextualized grammar activities

Each *Domino* pack contains a reader, and a MultiROM with:
- an excitingly dramatized audio recording of the story
- interactive games and activities to improve language skills

If you liked this Level Two *Domino*, read these:

War Horse
Michael Morpurgo

'We'll be friends, you and I. I'll call you Joey,' Albert said. 'I'll look after you. We'll always be friends, I promise.'

Albert Narracott, a farmer's boy, makes this promise to his horse, Joey, in Devon, England. But this is before the First World War, and before Joey leaves for France to become a war horse. What happens to Joey in the British army? What will the Germans and the French do to him when they find him? And how will Albert find Joey again?

V is for Vampire
Lesley Thompson

When Viktor Sarav takes a job at Ballantine's, Angie and her brother Don – the young owners of the New York fashion company – are pleased. But soon there are strange deaths in the company. Is there a vampire at work at Ballantine's? Vera Donato, a company director with secrets to hide, is against Viktor. But Ed Valdemar, the company lawyer, trusts him. Who is right?

	CEFR	Cambridge Exams	IELTS	TOEFL iBT	TOEIC
Level 3	B1	PET	4.0	57-86	550
Level 2	A2–B1	KET-PET	3.0-4.0	–	390
Level 1	A1–A2	YLE Flyers/KET	3.0	–	225
Starter & Quick Starter	A1	YLE Movers	1.0–2.0	–	–

You can find details and a full list of books and teachers' resources on our website: www.oup.com/elt/gradedreaders